Asma Shah

I left my homeland because I do not want to stay in the den of snakes and scorpions. I do not call that courage. I call it stupidity. I have this freedom of speech because I am not in my family and Pakistan

"Pak-is-Satan".

I was born in a Muslim Sunni Syed family. In Pakistan Quran, education taught to Muslim children in Arabic but many few understand the meaning. The majority of Muslims are not aware of the inhumane teachings of Islam.

I was, given all Islamic education and being born in a Syed family, I saw in how many ways Islam,

Manjeet Singh

I was born in Northern India. My family is an educated Sikh Punjabi family. In my family men are taught at a young age to work hard and succeed. I was in media since my college days.

My first marriage was according to my parents will, with Balbir Kaur on 27 June 1984. Her attitude was all the time with me and my family uncontrollable because most of the time she was abusing my parents, sisters and brothers with filthy words.

At first I thought it is due to mental incompatibility. I am not sorry to say that she had relations with her brother in law. I came to know after we had a daughter, but her illicit

Institute of Terrorism ISLAM

Asma Shah & Manjeet Singh

Order this book online at www.trafford.com/07-1192
or email orders@trafford.com

Most Trafford titles are also available at major online book retailers.

Note for Librarians: A cataloguing record for this book is available from Library and Archives Canada at www.collectionscanada.ca/amicus/index-e.html

ISBN: 978-1-4251-3213-2

www.trafford.com

North America & international
toll-free: 1 888 232 4444 (USA & Canada)
phone: 250 383 6864 ♦ fax: 250 383 6804
email: info@trafford.com

The United Kingdom & Europe
phone: +44 (0)1865 722 113 ♦ local rate: 0845 230 9601
facsimile: +44 (0)1865 722 868 ♦ email: info.uk@trafford.com

10 9 8 7 6 5 4 3 2 1

EK ONG KAR, SAT NAM, SIRI WHAHE GURU

WHAHE GURU KA KHALSA WHAHE GURU KI FATHE

This book will help you understand why Muslims are behind the deadly deeds. This book provides the reader with an extremely valuable insight into what the Islamic holy book, the Quran, teaches.

Truth is that Islam is giving birth to terrorism. You fight one terrorist group; ten more emerge from beneath the rock.

The actions of Islamic terrorist groups operating throughout the world are well known. These treacherous people have spared no one. When a Muslim declares that Islam is a religion of peace, he/she is ignorant of Quran. Alternatively, is deceitfully thinking of this peace, as it extends only to those within the Muslim Community. The deceit is that they will not tell you exactly what they mean.

48:29

سورة 84 - سورة الـ ف تح

VICTORY

مُّحَمَّدٌ رَّسُولُ اللَّهِ وَالَّذِينَ مَعَهُ أَشِدَّاء عَلَى الْكُفَّارِ رُحَمَاء
بَيْنَهُمْ تَرَاهُمْ رُكَّعًا سُجَّدًا يَبْتَغُونَ فَضْلًا مِّنَ اللَّهِ وَرِضْوَانًا
سِيمَاهُمْ فِي وُجُوهِهِم مِّنْ أَثَرِ السُّجُودِ ذَلِكَ مَثَلُهُمْ فِي
التَّوْرَاةِ وَمَثَلُهُمْ فِي الْإِنجِيلِ كَزَرْعٍ أَخْرَجَ شَطْأَهُ فَآزَرَهُ
فَاسْتَغْلَظَ فَاسْتَوَى عَلَى سُوقِهِ يُعْجِبُ الزُّرَّاعَ لِيَغِيظَ بِهِمُ
الْكُفَّارَ وَعَدَ اللَّهُ الَّذِينَ آمَنُوا وَعَمِلُوا الصَّالِحَاتِ مِنْهُم
مَّغْفِرَةً وَأَجْرًا عَظِيمًا

Muhammad is the apostle of Allah; and those who are with him are strong against Unbelievers, (but) compassionate amongst each other. Thou wilt see them bow and prostrate themselves (in prayer), seeking Grace from Allah and (His) Good Pleasure. On their faces are their marks, (being) the traces of their prostration. This is their similitude in the Taurat; and their similitude in the Gospel is like a seed which sends forth its blade, then makes it strong; it then becomes thick, and it stands on its own stem, (filling) the sowers with wonder and delight. As a result, it fills the Unbelievers with rage at them. Allah has promised those among them who believe and do righteous deeds forgiveness, and a great Reward.

سورة التوبة - سورة 9

REPENTANCE

فَإِذَا انسَلَخَ الأَشْهُرُ الْحُرُمُ فَاقْتُلُواْ الْمُشْرِكِينَ حَيْثُ وَجَدتُّمُوهُمْ وَخُذُوهُمْ وَاحْصُرُوهُمْ وَاقْعُدُواْ لَهُمْ كُلَّ مَرْصَدٍ فَإِن تَابُواْ وَأَقَامُواْ الصَّلاَةَ وَآتَوُاْ الزَّكَاةَ فَخَلُّواْ سَبِيلَهُمْ إِنَّ اللّهَ غَفُورٌ رَّحِيمٌ

But when the forbidden months are past, then fight and slay the Pagans wherever ye find them, an seize them, beleaguer them, and

by Allah and His Apostle, nor acknowledge the religion of Truth, (even if they are) of the People of the Book, until they pay the Jizya with willing submission, and feel themselves subdued

Muhammad commanded Muslims to spread Islam through Jihad. Muslims also commanded to take any land such as Israel. Muslims believe that they are Mujahedeen, or "holy warriors of Allah". Their goal is to establish the entire world as an Islamic state that conforms to Islamic laws.

Islam does not allow Muslims to leave Islam or else risk his or her life. Among other things, the religion of Islam is a brainwashing religion, and that is why so many Muslims turn into crazy Mindless zombies. Islamic law encourages Muslims to convert others.

The Quran says that Muhammad was to show the mercy of God to the world. Nevertheless, he became a military dictator, attacking, killing and taking plunder to finance his empire. How is that showing mercy? Muhammad was in fact an ambitious terrorist, criminal and murderer, whose entire life based on victimizing innocents and indulging in mindless violence.

their own, who are dedicated to attacking persons who hold different beliefs.

A sick and fearful religion system seeks to be correct, remove or restricted to Islamic countries. Fundamentalist have occupied and are trying to keep Muslims under full control because lots are secretly leaving Islam. Many Women are raising their voices and are confident now, to stand for their rights but many are still helpless. Some give hope because of life threat to them and their children. A lot is still to be uncovered.

The founder of the religion

Prophet Mohammad

A Terrorist

Crime exists in every society. We are focusing on the violent actions Muslims carry out. Muslims who carry out bombings, in which hundreds of innocents died, do so because they feel they are attacking Islamic enemies and have Allah's sanction to do so.

We are focusing on terrorism based upon what Muhammad taught and did. We are focusing on

Muslims, who for the sake of Islam committing violent acts of terrorism.

However, we want all our readers to know that we are fully aware of what we are writing. Islam has become one of the major world religions, founded by the Mohammed in Arabia in the 7th century AD. Muslims believe that idol-worship is a sin. Allah, which means God in Arabic, viewed as the sole God the creator, the sustainer, and restorer of the world.

Muhammad the son of Amina and Abdull Muttalib, he was born in the city of Mecca, in Arabia. His father died before he was born, so at the time of his birth, his mother, Amina, sent for his grandfather. His grandfather came and took him to the Kaba, (worship center) where he prayed for the infant and gave him the name of Muhammad.

Tradition says that, in those days nursing mothers, hired for infants. A woman named Halima, from the tribe of Bani Sad, had come to the city of Mecca in search of a child who needed a nurse. This was her means of employment. Therefore, Muhammad for, nursing was given to her. When Muhammad was two years old, Halima brought him back to his mother but begged her to let her keep him a while longer, because he had brought her so luck, so Amina agreed. As a young child, he tended the goats with his foster

Muhammad conceived his religion to satiate his lust for power, sex, and money. He was a terrorist that is why he taught the same lesson on the name of Allah. The Islamic reward for terror, kidnapping, and murder is Allah's Garden of Bliss, Paradise.

47:4

سورة 74 - سورة محمد

MUHAMMAD

فَإِذا لَقِيتُمُ الَّذِينَ كَفَرُوا فَضَرْبَ الرِّقَابِ حَتَّى إِذَا أَثْخَنتُمُوهُمْ فَشُدُّوا الْوَثَاقَ فَإِمَّا مَنًّا بَعْدُ وَإِمَّا فِدَاء حَتَّى تَضَعَ الْحَرْبُ أَوْزَارَهَا ذَلِكَ وَلَوْ يَشَاء اللَّهُ لَانتَصَرَ مِنْهُمْ وَلَكِن لِّيَبْلُوَ بَعْضَكُم بِبَعْضٍ وَالَّذِينَ قُتِلُوا فِي سَبِيلِ اللَّهِ فَلَن يُضِلَّ أَعْمَالَهُمْ

Therefore, when ye meet the Unbelievers (in fight), smite at their necks; At length, when ye have thoroughly subdued them, bind a bond firmly (on them): thereafter (is the time for) either generosity or ransom: Until the war lays down its burdens. Thus (are ye commanded):

The first Terrorist Attack Conquering Kaba

Eight years later Muhammad returned to Mecca. Muslim position was strong enough for he had gained many followers and converters to Islam. He felt that the Gods in the Kaba were evil, so he went to the Kaba and purified it by removing the various idols in the ancient, Arab shrine.

This shows he had no respect for other religions and he not only thought but also made others conceder by force that Islam is superior, what he says is the message of his Allah. Muhammad's followers became a threat to the local tribes and the rulers of the city. Muhammad gained followers by using force. The converters were warriors. To reject Allah and Islam was to invite death.

Kaba was already the most important sanctuary in pre-Muslim times in Arabia. It is located in Mecca. Muslims throughout the world direct their prayers toward the Kaba.

Muhammad claimed that it was a place built by Ibrahim. Muhammad made up historical references for the Kaba. Muhammad claimed that Ibrahim and Ishmael laid the foundations of the Kaba.

There are problems with this Muslim logic. First, there is no evidence that Abraham and Ishmael ever went to Mecca, or that they were the ones that originally built the Kaba. Apart from the statements of the Quran, Muslims are unable to provide any biblical or pre-Islamic evidence for this claim.

In Bukhari: A Hindu king sent a jar of ginger pickles to the Prophet. This shows that the Hindu Jat Raja ruled an adjacent area. Hindus, paint the crescent moon across the forehead that indicates symbol of the Siva. Since that symbol was associated with the Siva emblem in Kaba, so it grafted on the flag of Islam.

Historically, the Kaba used to be Temple of Lord Siva until the Muslim forces took control of Mecca. Hindu tradition associated with the Kaba is that of the sacred stream Ganga, (sacred waters of the Ganges River). Wherever there is Lord Siva, Ganga must co-exist. True to that association, a sacred fountain exists near the Kaba. This water is sacred because traditionally it regarded as Ganga. Muslims have a story built up that it was discovered by wife and son of Ibrahim and they say Abe Zam-Zam, meaning water to stop, in Arabic language.

Muslim pilgrims visiting the Kaba Temple go around it seven times. In no other mosque does the circumambulation prevail. Hindus invariably circumambulate around their deities.

This is yet another proof that the Kaba shrine is a pre-Islamic Hindu Shiva Temple where the Hindu practice of circumambulation, still meticulously observed. The practice of taking seven steps known as Saptapadi in Sanskrit is associated with Hindu marriage ceremony and fire worship. Muslims cannot do Hajj until they kiss the black stone this shows the power of Lord Shiva that without his permission they cannot go around his temple.

Hindu Lord Shiva

The Trishul in hand of the Lord
Is like the Arabic text ALLAH

Islam

Arabic text ALLAH

The Kaba, for Muslims the most revered sanctuary of Islam. Muhammad claimed that God ordained the Kaba as a sacred house. Muhammad claimed that it was the first temple ever built for humankind. He knew the importance of Kaba. Therefore, Muhammad wanted to conquer Kaba for Muslims on the name of Islam.

We will sagest Muslims to uncover the truth like Ghalib, a Muslim poet, warned not to lift the covers off the Kaba lest we might find an idol.

Accordingly, to Islam before Muhammad appeared, Kaba surrounded by 360 idols, and every Arab house had a god. The shapes and figures of the idols also made according to the fancy of the worshippers. Thus, Wadd, shaped like a man, Naila like a woman, so was Suwa. Yaghuth made in the shape of lion, Yauq like a horse and Nasr like a vulture. The greatest of these was Hubel. Besides Hubel, there was another idol called Shams placed on the roof of the Kaba. Besides idol-worship, they also worshipped the stars, the sun and the moon.

All this also confirms the presence of Hinduism. Arabs also believed in jinn (subtle beings), and some vague divinity with many offspring.

The major deities of the pre-Islamic era were:
Al-Lat, "the Goddess" worshiped in the shape of a square stone.
Al-Uzzah, "the Mighty" a goddess identified with the morning star and worshiped as a thigh-bone-shaped slab of granite between al Talf and Mecca.
Manat, the goddess of destiny, worshiped as a black stone on the road between Mecca and Medina.
Hubel, god of moon, worship connected with the Black Stone of the Kaba.

The stones said to have fallen from the sun, moon, stars, and planets and to represent cosmic

Al-Hajarul Aswad
Black stone

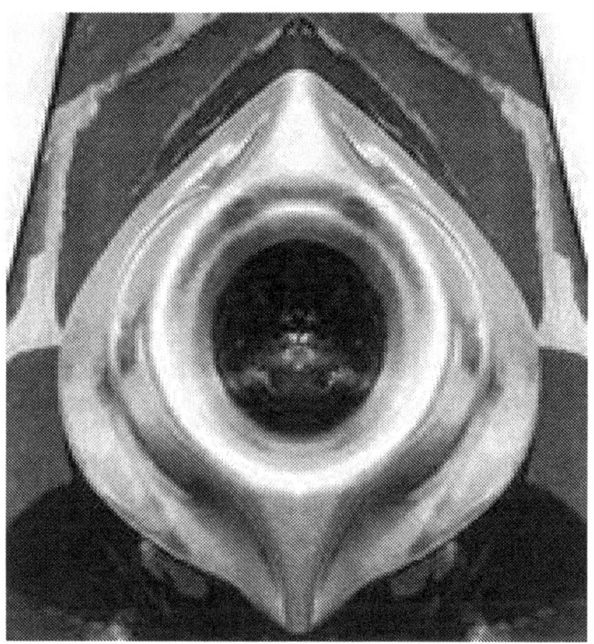

Muhammad Taught his followers To kill non-Muslims

They believe that their religion is above all others because the revelation to Muhammad was the last and final and the most accurate. Muhammad had established Islam as a social and political force. For most of the sixty-three years of his life, Muhammad was a merchant, then a prophet. He took up the sword late in his life. He was a warrior for ten years.

سورة 74 - سورة محمد

Muhammad

فَإِذا لَقِيتُمُ الَّذِينَ كَفَرُوا فَضَرْبَ الرِّقَابِ حَتَّى إِذَا أَثْخَنتُمُوهُمْ
فَشُدُّوا الْوَثَاقَ فَإِمَّا مَنًّا بَعْدُ وَإِمَّا فِدَاء حَتَّى تَضَعَ الْحَرْبُ
أَوْزَارَهَا ذَلِكَ وَلَوْ يَشَاء اللَّهُ لَانتَصَرَ مِنْهُمْ وَلَكِن لِّيَبْلُوَ بَعْضَكُم
بِبَعْضٍ وَالَّذِينَ قُتِلُوا فِي سَبِيلِ اللَّهِ فَلَن يُضِلَّ أَعْمَالَهُمْ

Now when you meet the unbelievers, strike at their necks. Until, when you have slaughtered them sufficiently, tie fast the bonds; then afterwards (set them free) either by grace or by ransom, till the war lays down its loads, so it shall be. And if God had willed, He could have avenged Himself upon them, but it was so that He may try some of you by others. And those who are killed in the way of God, He will never send their works astray

Muhammad told his followers to attack the Jews and Christians. If, they humble themselves, submit to the Muslims, but choose to remain Christian or Jewish, then they had to pay the Muslims. To live they pay a special tax. This was not to support the state it was to compensate the Muslims.

The same remedy still some Muslim countries are practicing, they take aids and charity to help the needy but the purpose is to invest in Terrorism.

Muhammad was crime boss, making others pay for protection, except it was Christians and Jews who really needed protection from the Muslims.

Here is the verse in the Quran that tells Muslims to attack and kill non-Muslim

Muhammad had an agreement with a number of Arab tribes, for peace. Allah gave Muhammad a revelation, allowing him to break the agreement with the Arab pagan and attack them after the four sacred months were over.

Muhammad had gained power, and things changed. Now Allah permitted, Muhammad to lie, break his agreement, and make war upon the pagans.

Muhammad's circumstances changed, and his Allah changed again.

سورة التوبة - سورة 9

Repentance

فَإِذَا انسَلَخَ الأَشْهُرُ الْحُرُمُ فَاقْتُلُواْ الْمُشْرِكِينَ حَيْثُ وَجَدتُّمُوهُمْ
وَخُذُوهُمْ وَاحْصُرُوهُمْ وَاقْعُدُواْ لَهُمْ كُلَّ مَرْصَدٍ فَإِن تَابُواْ
وَأَقَامُواْ الصَّلاَةَ وَآتَوُاْ الزَّكَاةَ فَخَلُّواْ سَبِيلَهُمْ إِنَّ اللّهَ غَفُورٌ
رَّحِي

Then, when the sacred months have passed away, kill the idolaters wherever you find them, and take them, and confine them, and sit for them at every place of ambush. Then, if they repent, and establish the Prayer, and pay the Due-Alms, leave alone their way; God is Forgiving, Merciful

Muhammad conquered by force and killed on the name of jihad. Muhammad also taught that Muslims who leave the Islamic faith are to be murdered. He further taught that a Muslim, who commits this type of murder, would be doing God's service. Those Muslims will, be rewarded in the Heaven.

Muhammad and his followers did many battles. Critics say that his wars went well beyond self-defense. Muslim commentators, however, argue that he fought only to defend his community against Islam his religion and that he insisted on humane rules of warfare.

Muhammad and his followers believed only Islam was the best religion and they wanted Islam all over, for them there was no respect or regard for any other religion.

سورة الأنفال - سورة 8

The Spoils

إِن تَسْتَفْتِحُواْ فَقَدْ جَاءكُمُ الْفَتْحُ وَإِن تَنتَهُواْ فَهُوَ خَيْرٌ لَّكُمْ وَإِن تَعُودُواْ نَعُدْ وَلَن تُغْنِيَ عَنكُمْ فِئَتُكُمْ شَيْئًا وَلَوْ كَثُرَتْ وَأَنَّ اللّهَ مَعَ الْمُؤْمِنِينَ

If you sought decision, then decision has come to you; now if you give over, it will be better for you, but if you repeat, We shall also repeat, and your host will not avail you at all, how numerous it may be, for God is with the Believers

سورة البقرة - سورة 2

The Cow

تُسْأَلُ إِنَّا أَرْسَلْنَاكَ بِالْحَقِّ بَشِيرًا وَنَذِيرًا وَلاَ عَنْ أَصْحَابِ الْجَحِيمِ

We have sent thee with the truth, as a bearer of good news and as a

Fight those who do not believe in God, nor in the Last Day, nor do they forbid what God and His Messenger have forbidden, nor do they practice the religion of truth, from among those who were given the Book, until they pay tribute out of hand, duly humbled

وَقَالَتِ الْيَهُودُ عُزَيْرٌ ابْنُ اللّهِ وَقَالَتْ النَّصَارَى الْمَسِيحُ ابْنُ اللّهِ ذَلِكَ قَوْلُهُم بِأَفْوَاهِهِمْ يُضَاهِؤُونَ قَوْلَ الَّذِينَ كَفَرُواْ مِن قَبْلُ قَاتَلَهُمُ اللّهُ أَنَّى يُؤْفَكُونَ

And the Jews say, `Ezra is the son of God', and the Christians say, `Messiah is the son of God'; that is their utterance with their mouths; they imitate the utterance of the unbelievers before them; God destroy them; how perverted they are

The Muslims were clearly the dominant force in Arabia. His converts grew as his influence increased, and so did large scale of warfare. Muhammad's community grew rapidly in power Muhammad's authority became important.

Muhammad had none of what today called civil authority. He had proclaimed himself a prophet, but it was not at all clear that a prophet must always have a successor.

Muhammad emerged as the political leader of an expanding community. Muhammad told his followers not to make non-Muslims friend

In 619, both Muhammad's wife Khadijah and his uncle Abu Talib died. This year was, known as a year of sorrows. Muhammad's own clan withdrew their protection of him. Muslims patiently endured hunger and persecution.

Wives of Muhammad

Muhammad was married to number of wives. The exact number is not certain but it has believed that he had twelve or thirteen wives in all.

The polygamy he practiced, and which he allowed to Muslims in general, is often been looked upon as a further weakness in his character.

Muhammad was a cleaver man. He used to do the trading for her so he got confidence of Khadija in no time, she got impressed with the honesty and she found a person as life partner.

Muhammad married her so there was no need to work. Khadija was 40 Muhammad was 25. She was fifteen years older.

Muhammad was successful in getting rich after marring Khadija but how long could stay off from his sex life so the next step was to go in mountains where Khadija was not able to come. Khadija was a mature woman and to fool her Muhammad needed a strong answer to stay away from her so he thought of securing his future by becoming a Prophet.

Muhammad developed his image of an honest man. Now he started to make people stupid with all the stupidities that he said. Muhammad benefited immensely from his lies and his believers started from his home.

He took advantage of his faithful wife Khadija as he planned. He used Khadija as his first step to successes in becoming a prophet of a Terrorist religion Islam.

A brief examination of his marriages after the death of Khadija will assist us to draw our own conclusions. After her death, he married Aisha, then Hafsa. Later he married more wives. The status of Maria al-Qibtiyya is much, disputed; she may have been a slave, a freed slave, a concubine, or a wife.

Khadijah

Khadijah was his faithful and upright first wife. She was a forty-year-old rich widow, fifteen years older than Muhammad was.

Khadijah was the first to accept Muhammad as a prophet and stood staunchly behind him through many years of persecution and turmoil in Mecca. While she lived, he married no other wife.

Accounts differ as to his next marriage. Most say that it was to Sawada bint Zama; some say it was to Aisha.

Khadija died in 619 AD

Sawada

Therefore, in the same year that Khadija died Muhammad married Sawda binty Zam'ah, a widow with a son. She was over thirty years of age.

At about the same time he betrothed to Aisha, whom he married formally three years later in Medina, but until she was nine years, he married Umm Salama.

Zaynab bint Jahsh

Muhammad married Zaynab bint Jahsh at Medina.

Aisha

Aisha, she was daughter Abu Baker. Muhammad's closest, friend. He became the first Calipha. Muhammad married her when she was six years old and he consummated his marriage when she was nine years old.

The thought of an old man aroused by a child is one of the most disturbing thoughts. Muhammad had sex with 9-year-old child; it is the proof that Muhammad was not a prophet but an evil man and a Terrorist.

This is the nature of blind faith, that Muslims brush it away and bring all sorts of excuses to justify this shameful act. She was a little girl, not yet reached the age of puberty.

Sahih Bukhari Volume 7, Book 62, Number 90

Narrated Aisha:
When the Prophet married me, my mother came to me and made me enter the house of the Prophet and nothing surprised me but the

coming of Allah's Apostle to me in the forenoon. The following is also interesting because it demonstrates that she was just a kid playing with her dolls.

Sahih Bukhari Volume 8, Book 73, Number 151

Narrated 'Aisha:
I used to play with the dolls in the presence of the Prophet, and my girl friends used to play with me. When Allah's Apostle used to enter my dwelling place they used to hide themselves, but the Prophet would call them to join and play with me. The playing with the dolls and similar images forbidden in Islam, but was allowed for Aisha at that time, as she was a little girl, not yet reached the age of puberty.

Some Muslims claim it was Abu Baker, who approached Muhammad asking him to marry his daughter. This is of course not true and here is the proof.

Sahih Bukhari 187

Narrated 'Ursa:
The Prophet asked Abu Bakr for 'Aisha's hand in marriage. Abu Bakr said "But I am your brother." The Prophet said, "You are my brother in Allah's religion and His Book, but she (Aisha) is lawful for me to marry."

Shia Muslims deny most of the traditions narrated above. They take a very dim view of Aisha and of her father, Abu Baker.

They deny that Abu Baker was close to Muhammad; they do not believe that Aisha was Muhammad's favorite wife. He defended her when she was, accused of adultery.

Once Aisha separated from the rest of the party while on a trip, and brought back by one of Muhammad's companions, Shafwan ibn Muatthal. Since she had been alone with another man, people gossiped and said that she must be having an affair.

Muhammad refused to repudiate her, and then received a revelation that four eyewitnesses were necessary to prove adultery. This proves that Muhammad had a devil mind instead of believing his wife he wanted proves.

This shows the respect of women in Islam. This uncovers the status of a wife in Islam. Muhammad cheated his first wife Khadija so he had the same thought for his wife Aisha, no matter he said to her how much he loves her.

سورة 42 - سورة الـ نور

The Light

وَآتُواْ النَّسَاء صَدُقَاتِهِنَّ نِحْلَةً فَإِن طِبْنَ لَكُمْ عَن شَيْءٍ مِّنْهُ
نَفْسًا فَكُلُوهُ هَنِيئًا مَّرِيئًا

And those who accuse chaste women, then do not bring four witnesses, flog them with eighty stripes, and do not accept their testimony ever, for they are the transgressors.

In his last illness, Muhammad sought her company and died with his head in her lap.

Muhammad married widows of Muslims killed in battles

Hafsa

Hafsa was the daughter of Umar, another close friend; her husband killed at Badar. Muhammad married Hafsa when the Muslims were engaged in constant warfare in 624-629.

He linked by marriage to two of his chief lieutenants Abu Baker, who was to lead the Muslims after Muhammad's death, and Omar, who became calipha after Abu Bakr.

Zaynab bint Jahsh

Even while Zaid was still married to Zaynab, it was the will of Allah that Muhammad should be married to her and he is reproved for encouraging Zaid to remain married when Allah had something else in mind.

Muhammad steadfastly encouraged Zaid to keep her as his wife to acquit of the charge that he caused the divorce and took advantage of it to satisfy his own whims and desires. Quran exposes itself to critical review in its sanction of the whole affair.

سورة 33 - سورة الأحزاب

The Confederates

وَإِذْ تَقُولُ لِلَّذِي أَنْعَمَ اللَّهُ عَلَيْهِ وَأَنْعَمْتَ عَلَيْهِ أَمْسِكْ عَلَيْكَ
زَوْجَكَ وَاتَّقِ اللَّهَ وَتُخْفِي فِي نَفْسِكَ مَا اللَّهُ مُبْدِيهِ وَتَخْشَى
النَّاسَ وَاللَّهُ أَحَقُّ أَن تَخْشَاهُ فَلَمَّا قَضَى زَيْدٌ مِّنْهَا وَطَرًا
زَوَّجْنَاكَهَا لِكَيْ لَا يَكُونَ عَلَى الْمُؤْمِنِينَ حَرَجٌ فِي أَزْوَاجِ
أَدْعِيَائِهِمْ إِذَا قَضَوْا مِنْهُنَّ وَطَرًا وَكَانَ أَمْرُ اللَّهِ مَفْعُولًا

This censure may well be unfounded. Zaynab was his own cousin, Muhammad had known her for many years, and it is hard to believe that after all this time he suddenly infatuated by an opportune view of her beauty.

There is therefore a strong presumption that in the case of Zaynab bint Jahsh, Muhammad was not carried away by passion . . . it is unlikely that he was swept off his feet by the physical attractiveness of Zaynab.

Rayhanah

She was one of the women captured after the sedge of the Banu Quraydhah, the Jewish tribe near Medina subsequently massacred for colluding with the Quraysh.

He invited her to be his wife; but she declined and chose to remain his slave. She also declined the summons to conversion, and continued in the Jewish faith, at which Muhammad was much concerned.
However, that she afterwards embraced Islam. She did not many years survive her unhappy fate.

Having just witnessed the butchery of her husband and all her male relatives, it is hardly surprising to find that she had shown repugnance towards Islam when she was captured and clung to Judaism.

Many Muslims defend Muhammad's polygamous marriages by saying that most of his wives were divorcees or widows. It should, be remembered that the two Jewish women attached to him were only widows because Muhammad's followers had slaughtered their husbands just before they were brought into his camp.

Umm Salama Hind bint Abi Umayya

He married captives widowed when their cities were, taken.

Safiyya bint Huyayy

Muhammad said he married Safiyya to save her from slavery.

Juwayriya bint al-Harith

Juwayriya of the Banu Khuzah defeated in an attack by Muhammad in the fifth year of the Hijrah. Her marriage became a ransom for the whole tribe who were, released immediately.

The young Aisha, becoming patently jealous of the increasing number of wives added to the household, commented:

She was a most beautiful woman. She captivated every man who saw her. She came to the Apostle to ask his help in the matter. As soon as I saw her at the door of my room, I took a dislike for her, for I knew that he would see her as I saw her. He married for political reasons.

Umm Habibah Ramla

Umm Habibah, who had also immigrated to Abyssinia, and a Jewess Safiyah, who lost her father Huyayy, her husband Kinanah, and both her brothers during Muhammad's assault on the fortress at Khaibar.

Maria al-Qibtiyya

Maria was the mother of Ibrahim, a short-lived son by Muhammad

Maymuna bint al-Harith

Maymunah was a slave girl, sent to him by the ruler of Egypt. He married her; this was his last marriage to a widow.

The Jealousy between Muhammad's Wives

At least nine of Muhammad's wives survived after him. The Quran only allows Muslims up to four wives at a time.

4.3

سورة النساء - سورة 4

WOMEN

وَإِنْ خِفْتُمْ أَلاَّ تُقْسِطُواْ فِي الْيَتَامَى فَانكِحُواْ مَا طَابَ لَكُم مِّنَ
النِّسَاء مَثْنَى وَثُلاَثَ وَرُبَاعَ فَإِنْ خِفْتُمْ أَلاَّ تَعْدِلُواْ فَوَاحِدَةً أَوْ مَا
مَلَكَتْ أَيْمَانُكُمْ ذَلِكَ أَدْنَى أَلاَّ تَعُولُواْ

If ye fear that ye shall not be able to deal justly with the orphans, marry women of your choice, two, or three, or four; but if ye fear that ye shall not be able to deal justly (with them), then only one, or (a captive) that your right hands possess. That will be more suitable, to prevent you from doing injustice.

However, Muhammad was entitled to as many as he was chose until the Quran forbade him to take any more

33.52

سورة 33 - سورة الأحزاب

The Confederates

لَا يَحِلُّ لَكَ النِّسَاء مِن بَعْدُ وَلَا أَن تَبَدَّلَ بِهِنَّ مِنْ أَزْوَاجٍ وَلَوْ أَعْجَبَكَ حُسْنُهُنَّ إِلَّا مَا مَلَكَتْ يَمِينُكَ وَكَانَ اللَّهُ عَلَى كُلِّ شَيْءٍ رَّقِيبًا

It is not lawful for thee (to marry more) women after this, nor to change them for (other) wives, even though their beauty attract thee, except any thy right hand should possess (as handmaidens): and Allah doth watch over all things.

As mentioned, polygamy, as sanctioned and approved in the Quran, is been regarded in non-Muslim circles as one of the weaknesses of Islam. Sensitive to any charge against the infallibility of the teaching of their religion and the practice of their prophet, Muslim writers invariably seek to justify polygamy.

The argument usually put forward is that polygamy is perfectly in order provided the wives equal treatment. As Muhammad had many wives he is often strongly defended against the allegation that he could not have treated them equally.

The surest way to discover the truth of the matter is not to ask whether he himself persuaded that they were so treated, but to enquire from his wives whether they ever felt any jealousy for one another or whether their very number in the household caused any friction.

There are many traditions recording that Muhammad's wives were jealous of one another and not always pleased with him either. Indeed, on one occasion he kept aloof from them for a while and threatened to divorce them all.

Aisha and Hafsah expressed some displeasure to Muhammad over the length of time he spent with Zaynab bint Jahsh. Being the youngest of his wives, it is not surprising that they were usually at the heart of Muhammad's domestic problems.

Indeed Umar, Hafsah's father, not only found that Muhammad's wives argued with him quite regularly but even suspected that his daughter envied Aisha as well because Muhammad clearly regarded her as his favorite wife.

He prompted to enquire into the relationship between Hafsah and Muhammad by a sharp remark made by his own wife on one occasion to him:

Sahih -Bukhari, Vol. 6, p. 406.

She said, how strange you are, O son of al-Khattab! You don't want to be argued with whereas your daughter, Hafsa surely, argues with Allah's Apostle so much that he remains angry for a full day, Umar then reported how he at once put on his outer garment and went to Hafsa and said to her O my daughter! Do you argue with Allah's Apostle so that he remains angry the whole day? Hafsa answered By Allah, we argue with him. Umar said Know that I warn you of Allah's punishment and the anger of Allah's Apostle. O my daughter! Don't be betrayed by the one who is proud of her beauty because of the love of Allah's Apostle for her Aisha

It was Muhammad's custom to spend one day at a time with his wives in order but on one occasion, the irrepressible Hafsah discovered him with Mariyah in her own apartment on the day properly reserved for her alone.

When, finally, Mariyah left the quarters and Hafsah entered, she said to Muhammad, I have seen who was here and it is an insult to me.

Muhammad realized that such deep lying jealousy might even move Hafsah to other wives, what she had seen. In an attempt to please her, Muhammad promised that he would not go unto Mariyah if she would only refrain from not telling what she had seen.

Hafsah could not keep her promise as jealousy continued to affect her disposition and that she discussed the matter with Aisha.

The only thing that omits from the story is the statement made by all the commentators who record it that promise made by Muhammad was actually in the form of an oath. They add that Muhammad was later, freed from this oath by a Quran revelation:

66 سورة - الـ تحريـ م سورة

PROHIBITION

يَا أَيُّهَا النَّبِيُّ لِمَ تُحَرِّمُ مَا أَحَلَّ اللَّهُ لَكَ تَبْتَغِي مَرْضَاتَ أَزْوَاجِكَ وَاللَّهُ غَفُورٌ رَّحِيمٌ

O Prophet! Why hold thou to be forbidden that which Allah has made lawful to thee? Thou seek to please thy consorts but Allah is Oft-Forgiving, Most Merciful

قَدْ فَرَضَ اللَّهُ لَكُمْ تَحِلَّةَ أَيْمَانِكُمْ وَاللَّهُ مَوْلَاكُمْ وَهُوَ الْعَلِيمُ الْحَكِيمُ

Allah has already ordained for you, (O men), the dissolution of your oaths (in some cases): and Allah is your Protector, and He is full of Knowledge and Wisdom

Bukhari says that these verses refer to the incident where Muhammad told that the honey he had eaten with Zaynab smelt like a bitter herb.

Unfortunately, the Quran is somewhat vague at this point, saying only that the sanction to dissolve the oath arose out of the disclosure by one of Muhammad's wives to another of a matter of confidence told by him to the first.

66.3

سورة 66 - سورة الـ تحريـ م

PROHIBITION

وَإِذْ أَسَرَّ النَّبِيُّ إِلَى بَعْضِ أَزْوَاجِهِ حَدِيثًا فَلَمَّا نَبَّأَتْ بِهِ وَأَظْهَرَهُ اللَّهُ عَلَيْهِ عَرَّفَ بَعْضَهُ وَأَعْرَضَ عَن بَعْضٍ فَلَمَّا نَبَّأَهَا بِهِ قَالَتْ مَنْ أَنبَأَكَ هَذَا قَالَ نَبَّأَنِيَ الْعَلِيمُ الْخَبِيرُ

When the Prophet disclosed a matter of confidence to one of his consorts, and she then divulged it (to another), and Allah made it known to him, he confirmed part thereof and repudiated a part. Then when he told her thereof, she said, "Who told thee this?" He said, He told me who knows and is well-acquainted (with all things).

This could refer to either story and, although Bukhari confirms that, the two wives spoken of where the provocative young consorts Hafsah and Aisha (Sahih -Bukhari, Vol. 6, and p. 408.

Quran's treatment of the matter that makes it probable that the incident with Mariyah is really the one referred.

Firstly, if the oath spoken of was purely that relating to honey, it is hard to believe that such an issue would have been made of it in the Quran. The discreet omission of factual details in the Quran passage, however, tends even more to support the suggestion that a more sensitive matter was behind it.

Secondly, Quran adds that Muhammad confirmed a part of the allegation made by the spouse and repudiated a part.

Thirdly, the same verse states plainly that a matter purely between Muhammad and one of his wives was, disclosed to another.

This is inconsistent with the honey story as Aisha and Hafsah were both well aware of the matter all along, having mutually conspired to mislead Muhammad.

It does indeed seem that Sure 66.1-2 was a convenient revelation to enable Muhammad to break his vow not to go to Mariyah again.

سورة 66 - سورة الـ تحريـ م

PROHIBITION

يَا أَيُّهَا النَّبِيُّ لِمَ تُحَرِّمُ مَا أَحَلَّ اللَّهُ لَكَ تَبْتَغِي مَرْضَاتَ أَزْوَاجِكَ وَاللَّهُ غَفُورٌ رَّحِيمٌ

O Prophet! Why holdest thou to be forbidden that which Allah has made lawful to thee? Thou seekest to please thy consorts. But Allah is Oft Forgiving, Most Merciful

قَدْ فَرَضَ اللَّهُ لَكُمْ تَحِلَّةَ أَيْمَانِكُمْ وَاللَّهُ مَوْلَاكُمْ وَهُوَ الْعَلِيمُ الْحَكِيمُ

Allah has already ordained for you, (O men), the dissolution of your oaths (in some cases): and Allah is your Protector, and He is Full of Knowledge and Wisdom.

If God sanctions the breaking of a vow by one of his apostles, how can we be sure that he will be faithful to his own promises and oaths are sacred things, but Sure 66.1-2 seems to undermine the whole purpose and value of oaths. Shortly after this, a timely revelation in the Quran gave Muhammad the right to abandon the fixed sequence he had followed with his wives up to this time.

33.51

سورة 33 - سورة الأحزاب

The Confederates

تُرْجِي مَن تَشَاء مِنْهُنَّ وَتُؤْوِي إِلَيْكَ مَن تَشَاء وَمَنِ ابْتَغَيْتَ
مِمَّنْ عَزَلْتَ فَلَا جُنَاحَ عَلَيْكَ ذَلِكَ أَدْنَى أَن تَقَرَّ أَعْيُنُهُنَّ وَلَا
يَحْزَنَّ وَيَرْضَيْنَ بِمَا آتَيْتَهُنَّ كُلُّهُنَّ وَاللَّهُ يَعْلَمُ مَا فِي قُلُوبِكُمْ
وَكَانَ اللَّهُ عَلِيمًا حَلِيمًا

Thou mayest defer (the turn of) any of them that thou pleases, and thou mayest receive any thou pleases and there is no blame on thee if thou invite one whose (turn) thou had set aside. This were nether to the cooling of the eyes, the prevention of their grief, and their satisfaction - that of all of them - with that which thou hast to give them: and Allah knows (all) that is in your hearts: and Allah is All-Knowing, Most Forbearing

Aisha had openly complained of her jealousy towards those women are not named who had offered themselves to Allah's Messenger.

Sahih Muslim, Vol. 2, p. 748

Moreover, who gradually increased the size of the household as Muhammad under Quranic authority duly took them as his wives (presumably Aisha had at least Zaynab bint Jahsh and Juwayriyah in mind).

33.50

سورة 33 - سورة الأحزاب

THE CLANS

يَا أَيُّهَا النَّبِيُّ إِنَّا أَحْلَلْنَا لَكَ أَزْوَاجَكَ اللَّاتِي آتَيْتَ أُجُورَهُنَّ وَمَا مَلَكَتْ يَمِينُكَ مِمَّا أَفَاءَ اللَّهُ عَلَيْكَ وَبَنَاتِ عَمِّكَ وَبَنَاتِ عَمَّاتِكَ وَبَنَاتِ خَالِكَ وَبَنَاتِ خَالَاتِكَ اللَّاتِي هَاجَرْنَ مَعَكَ وَامْرَأَةً مُّؤْمِنَةً إِن وَهَبَتْ نَفْسَهَا لِلنَّبِيِّ إِنْ أَرَادَ النَّبِيُّ أَن يَسْتَنكِحَهَا خَالِصَةً لَّكَ مِن دُونِ الْمُؤْمِنِينَ قَدْ عَلِمْنَا مَا فَرَضْنَا عَلَيْهِمْ فِي أَزْوَاجِهِمْ وَمَا مَلَكَتْ أَيْمَانُهُمْ لِكَيْلَا يَكُونَ عَلَيْكَ حَرَجٌ وَكَانَ اللَّهُ غَفُورًا رَّحِيمًا

O Prophet! We have made lawful to thee thy wives to whom thou hast paid their dowers; and those whom thy right hand possesses out of the prisoners of war whom Allah has assigned to thee; and daughters of thy paternal uncles and aunts, and daughters of thy maternal uncles and aunts, who migrated (from Makka) with thee; and any believing woman who dedicates her soul to the Prophet if the Prophet wishes to wed her;- this only for thee, and not for the Believers (at large); We know what We have appointed for them as to their wives and the captives whom their right hands possess;- in order that there should be no difficulty for thee. And Allah is Oft Forgiving, Most Merciful.

advantage) over them. And Allah is Exalted in Power, Wise.

Everyone has the right of freedom to thought, conscience and religion. All human beings are born free and equal in dignity and rights. Everyone has the right to live life its own way. No one should, be subjected to torture or to cruel, inhuman or degrading treatment or punishment.

Men and women of full age, without any limitation due to race, nationality or religion, have the right to marry and to found a family. They are entitled to equal rights as to marriage, during marriage and at its dissolution.

Who is a woman in Islam? I will rather say what a woman, in Islam is. The women are toys. How can you respect a religion that forces women into polygamous marriages, mutilates their genitals, and subjects them to the humiliation of instant divorce?

How can anyone justify Islam's treatment of women, when it imprisons Afghans under blue shuttlecock burqas and makes Pakistani girls marry strangers against their will?

I personally suffered all this as a Muslim woman (daughter, sister, wife, all relations). Women in this religion do not have courage of uttering a word against her family or in laws.

How can a person respect a religion that forces women into polygamous marriages? Regardless of her skills or intelligence, she has to accept her man as not only the head of her household but also her owner.

According to Islamic teachings in the Quran and hadith, Muslim men are free to go where they want while Muslim women are confined to their houses, men do not need permission to leave the house from women, women do, men are not obligated to veil their beauty but Muslim women must.

A man may divorce his wife as easily as repeating the words "I divorce you" three times. A woman who wants to leave her husband must prove at least that he does not meet her needs.

A man may inherit twice as much as a woman. His testimony in matters of conflict is worth twice hers. It is in the Quran that a woman obeys her husband indefinitely. For the man conforming to the wishes of wife is an option.

A man may have sexual intercourse with his wife when and how he wants. Her refusal will invite the curses of angels and the wrath of her husband.

Apart from the wife of Muhammad's uncle Abu Lahab, and Zainab, one of Muhammad's wives to whom the Quran alluded, the Virgin Mary is the most important female character in the Quran.

The nineteenth sure of the Quran named after her, the only female name the Quran mentions. The other women whose stories narrated in the Quran are never, mentioned by name; rather they were called the wives of their respective husbands.

Among them are: Eve, the wife of Imran Sure Al Imran 3:35, the wife of the governor Sure Yusuf 12:30, Pharaoh's wife Sure al-Qasas 28:9, Lot's wife Sure al-Tahrim 66:10, Abraham's wife Sure Hud 11:71, and Noah's wife Sure al-Tahrim

سورة 82 - سورة الـ قصص

THE STORY

وَقَالَتِ امْرَأَتُ فِرْعَوْنَ قُرَّتُ عَيْنٍ لِّي وَلَكَ لَا تَقْتُلُوهُ عَسَى أَن
يَنفَعَنَا أَوْ نَتَّخِذَهُ وَلَدًا وَهُمْ لَا يَشْعُرُونَ

The wife of Pharaoh said: "(Here is) joy of the eye, for me and for thee: slay him not. It may be that he will be use to us, or we may adopt him as a son." And they perceived not (what they were doing)!

سورة 66 - سورة الـ تحريـ م

BANNING

ضَرَبَ اللَّهُ مَثَلًا لِّلَّذِينَ كَفَرُوا امْرَأَةَ نُوحٍ وَامْرَأَةَ لُوطٍ كَانَتَا
تَحْتَ عَبْدَيْنِ مِنْ عِبَادِنَا صَالِحَيْنِ فَخَانَتَاهُمَا فَلَمْ يُغْنِيَا عَنْهُمَا
مِنَ اللَّهِ شَيْئًا وَقِيلَ ادْخُلَا النَّارَ مَعَ الدَّاخِلِينَ

Allah sets forth, for an example to the Unbelievers, the wife of Noah and the wife of Lut: they were (respectively) under two of our righteous servants, but they were false to their (husbands), and they profited nothing before Allah on their account, but were told: "Enter ye the Fire along with (others) that enter!"

سورة هود - سورة 11

HUD

وَامْرَأَتُهُ قَآئِمَةٌ فَضَحِكَتْ فَبَشَّرْنَاهَا بِإِسْحَقَ وَمِن وَرَاء إِسْحَقَ يَعْقُوبَ

And his wife was standing (there), and she laughed: But we gave her glad tidings of Isaac, and after him, of Jacob.

The Quran pictures mother Mary as being disappointed over the fact that she gave birth to a female.

3:36

سورة آل عمران - سورة 3

THE FAMILY OF IMRAN

فَلَمَّا وَضَعَتْهَا قَالَتْ رَبِّ إِنِّي وَضَعْتُهَا أُنثَى وَاللّهُ أَعْلَمُ بِمَا وَضَعَتْ وَلَيْسَ الذَّكَرُ كَالأُنثَى وَإِنِّي سَمَّيْتُهَا مَرْيَمَ وِإِنِّي أُعِيذُهَا بِكَ وَذُرِّيَّتَهَا مِنَ الشَّيْطَانِ الرَّجِيمِ

When she was delivered, she said: "O my Lord! Behold! I am delivered of a female child!"- and Allah knew best what she brought forth- "And no wise is the male Like the female. I have named her Mary, and I commend her and her offspring to Thy protection from the Evil One, the Rejected."

Muhammad beat his wives

He (Muhammad bin- Qais) then reported that it was 'Aisha who had narrated this: Should I not narrate to you about myself and about the Messenger of Allah?

He said: Yes. She said: When it was my turn for Allah's Messenger to spend the night with me, he turned his side, put on his mantle and took off his shoes and placed them near his feet, and spread the corner of his shawl on his bed and then lay down till he thought that I had gone to sleep. He took hold of his mantle slowly and put on the shoes slowly, and opened the door and went out and then closed it lightly.

I covered my head, put on my veil and tightened my waist wrapper, and then went out following his steps until he reached Baqi. He stood there and he stood for a long time. He then lifted his hands three times, and then returned and I returned.

He hastened his steps and I hastened my steps. He ran and I too ran. He came (to the house) and I came (to the house). I, however, preceded him and I entered (the house), and as I lay down in the bed, he (Muhammad) entered the (house), and said: Why is it, O 'Aisha, that you are out of breath?

I said: There is nothing. He said: Tell me or the Subtle and the Aware would inform me. I said: Messenger of Allah, may my father and mother be ransom for you, and then I told him (the whole story). He said: Was it the darkness (of your shadow) that I saw in front of me? I said: Yes.

He struck me on the chest, which caused me pain, and then said: Did you think that Allah and His Apostle would deal unjustly?

Sahih Muslim: book 4, number 2127

Muhammad's companions Also, beat his wives And other women

Umar came forward, and when he had asked and been granted permission he found the Prophet sitting sad and silent with his wives around him. He told that he decided to say something, which would make the Prophet laugh, so he said, "Messenger of God, I wish you had seen the daughter of Kharija when she asked me for extra money and I got up and slapped her on the neck." God's messenger laughed and said, "They are

And know that ye are to meet Him (in the Hereafter), and give (these) good tidings to those who believe

Marriage in Islam binds a woman to one man but not the man to that woman. Men are, allowed, multiple wives and an unlimited number of slave girls.

Na Mahram

Na Mehram means anyone who is not immediately, related to you.

Islamic teaching forbids women to meet, talk, handshake, travel or have any relations like friendship and cannot even pray directly next to each other in mosques. Islam degrades women in all aspects of life to a level less than that of slaves.

Women are helpless and as a prisoner ultimately settle into a monotonous routine. Anger recedes, senses dull, spirit crushed. Women are a commodity meant for utilization and consumption in whichever way the owner, master deems fit.

Women must be kept out of the public view at all times, reserving her for use, under the absolute domination of men, for sexual pleasure and reproduction. According to Islamic values, woman is never, considered as a human being.

24:31

سورة 42 - سورة الـ نور

LIGHT

وَقُل لِّلْمُؤْمِنَاتِ يَغْضُضْنَ مِنْ أَبْصَارِهِنَّ وَيَحْفَظْنَ فُرُوجَهُنَّ
وَلَا يُبْدِينَ زِينَتَهُنَّ إِلَّا مَا ظَهَرَ مِنْهَا وَلْيَضْرِبْنَ بِخُمُرِهِنَّ عَلَى
جُيُوبِهِنَّ وَلَا يُبْدِينَ زِينَتَهُنَّ إِلَّا لِبُعُولَتِهِنَّ أَوْ آبَائِهِنَّ أَوْ آبَاء
بُعُولَتِهِنَّ أَوْ أَبْنَائِهِنَّ أَوْ أَبْنَاء بُعُولَتِهِنَّ أَوْ إِخْوَانِهِنَّ أَوْ بَنِي
إِخْوَانِهِنَّ أَوْ بَنِي أَخَوَاتِهِنَّ أَوْ نِسَائِهِنَّ أَوْ مَا مَلَكَتْ أَيْمَانُهُنَّ أَوِ
التَّابِعِينَ غَيْرِ أُوْلِي الْإِرْبَةِ مِنَ الرِّجَالِ أَوِ الطِّفْلِ الَّذِينَ لَمْ
يَظْهَرُوا عَلَى عَوْرَاتِ النِّسَاء وَلَا يَضْرِبْنَ بِأَرْجُلِهِنَّ لِيُعْلَمَ مَا
يُخْفِينَ مِن زِينَتِهِنَّ وَتُوبُوا إِلَى اللَّهِ جَمِيعًا أَيُّهَا الْمُؤْمِنُونَ
لَعَلَّكُمْ تُفْلِحُونَ

World is moving forward and all the secularist countries guarantee the rights of women, we cannot compare those reforms of women with the past time, we are no longer living in those so-called dark days but women in Islam does not have all rights.

Muhammad's Advice For Marriages

Narrated Jabir bin 'Abdullah: When I got married, Allah's Apostle said to me, "What type of lady have you married?" I replied, "I have married a matron' He said, "Why, don't you have a liking for the virgins, for fondling them?" Jabir also said, Allah's Apostle said, "why didn't you marry a young girl so that you might play with her and her with you?' Sahih al-Bukhari: volume 7, book 62, number 17, Khan

A man came to the Prophet and said, I have found a woman of rank and beauty, but she does not give birth to children. Should I marry her? He said, No. He came again to him, but he prohibited him. He came to him third time and he said, Marry women who are loving and very prolific.

Muhammad gave strong warnings to women who would not accommodate their husband or master's desire. Muhammad said: The best of your women is the one who if her husband looks at her she pleases him, and if he orders her something, she obeys, and if he is away, she keeps him in herself and his wealth.

Ali reported God's messenger as saying, "When a man calls his wife to satisfy his desire she must go to him even if she is occupied at the oven." Tirmidhi transmitted it.

Mishkat Al-Masabih: volume 2, p. 691 Narrated Abu Huraira: The Prophet said, "if a man invites his wife to sleep with him an she refuses to come to him, then angels send their curses on her till morning." Sahih al-Bukhari: volume 7, book 62, number 121

It is not only that a woman is quite similar to a baby-making factory; she is also a machine for enjoyment. In Islamic marriage, mutual love, understanding, companionship is not so important. The most important reason for marriage is the production of unlimited number of children without any regard for the health or the welfare of the women.

Islamic marriage rule permits a male Muslim to marry a woman of the Book (Jews and Christians, although some school of jurisprudence says that the Sabiun and the Zoroastrians are included too) though this type of inter-religious marriage is not encouraged.

However, Islam strictly forbids an Islamic woman to marry any male who is not a Muslim.

سورة البقرة - سورة 2

THE COW

وَلاَ تَنكِحُواْ الْمُشْرِكَاتِ حَتَّى يُؤْمِنَّ وَلأَمَةٌ مُّؤْمِنَةٌ خَيْرٌ مِّن مُّشْرِكَةٍ وَلَوْ أَعْجَبَتْكُمْ وَلاَ تُنكِحُواْ الْمُشِرِكِينَ حَتَّى يُؤْمِنُواْ وَلَعَبْدٌ مُّؤْمِنٌ خَيْرٌ مِّن مُّشْرِكٍ وَلَوْ أَعْجَبَكُمْ أُوْلَـئِكَ يَدْعُونَ إِلَى النَّارِ وَاللّهُ يَدْعُوَ إِلَى الْجَنَّةِ وَالْمَغْفِرَةِ بِإِذْنِهِ وَيُبَيِّنُ آيَاتِهِ لِلنَّاسِ لَعَلَّهُمْ يَتَذَكَّرُونَ

Do not marry unbelieving women (idolaters), until they believe: A slave woman who believes is better than an unbelieving woman, even though she allures you. Nor marry (your girls) to unbelievers until they believe: A man slave who believes is better than an unbeliever, even though he allures you. Unbelievers do (but) beckon you to the Fire. But Allah beckons by His Grace to the Garden (of bliss) and forgiveness, and makes His Signs clear to mankind: That they may celebrate His praise.

If an Islamic woman contravenes this divine rule, then her marriage is illegal and she is committing the act of Zina/adultery that may be punishable by 100 lashes or stoning to death.

Instead of promoting inter-religious harmony/tolerance, Islam is promoting hate and intolerance, and secondly, it is severely restricting the choice of an Islamic woman in the selection of her spouse.

disloyalty and ill-conduct, admonish them (first), (Next), refuse to share their beds, (And last) beat them (lightly); but if they return to obedience, seek not against them Means (of annoyance): For Allah is Most High, great (above you all).

عَلَّمَهُ اللّهُ فَلْيَكْتُبْ وَلْيُمْلِلِ الَّذِي عَلَيْهِ الْحَقُّ وَلْيَتَّقِ اللّهَ رَبَّهُ وَلاَ
يَبْخَسْ مِنْهُ شَيْئًا فَإن كَانَ الَّذِي عَلَيْهِ الْحَقُّ سَفِيهًا أَوْ ضَعِيفًا
أَوْ لاَ يَسْتَطِيعُ أَن يُمِلَّ هُوَ فَلْيُمْلِلْ وَلِيُّهُ بِالْعَدْلِ وَاسْتَشْهِدُواْ
شَهِيدَيْنِ من رِّجَالِكُمْ فَإِن لَّمْ يَكُونَا رَجُلَيْنِ فَرَجُلٌ وَامْرَأَتَانِ
مِمَّن تَرْضَوْنَ مِنَ الشُّهَدَاء أَن تَضِلَّ إْحْدَاهُمَا فَتُذَكِّرَ إِحْدَاهُمَا
الأُخْرَى وَلاَ يَأْبَ الشُّهَدَاء إِذَا مَا دُعُواْ وَلاَ تَسْأَمُوْاْ أَن تَكْتُبُوْهُ
صَغِيرًا أَو كَبِيرًا إِلَى أَجَلِهِ ذَلِكُمْ أَقْسَطُ عِندَ اللّهِ وَأَقْومُ لِلشَّهَادَةِ
وَأَدْنَى أَلاَّ تَرْتَابُواْ إِلاَّ أَن تَكُونَ تِجَارَةً حَاضِرَةً تُدِيرُونَهَا
بَيْنَكُمْ فَلَيْسَ عَلَيْكُمْ جُنَاحٌ أَلاَّ تَكْتُبُوهَا وَأَشْهِدُوْاْ إِذَا تَبَايَعْتُمْ وَلاَ
يُضَآرَّ كَاتِبٌ وَلاَ شَهِيدٌ وَإِن تَفْعَلُواْ فَإِنَّهُ فُسُوقٌ بِكُمْ وَاتَّقُواْ اللّهَ
وَيُعَلِّمُكُمُ اللّهُ وَاللّهُ بِكُلِّ شَيْءٍ عَلِيمٌ

O ye who believe! When ye deal with each other, in transactions involving future obligations in a fixed period of time, reduce them to writing Let a scribe write down faithfully as between the parties: let not the scribe refuse to write: as Allah Has taught him, so let him write. Let him who incurs the liability dictate, but let him fear His Lord Allah, and not diminish aught of what he owes. If they party liable is mentally deficient, or weak, or unable Himself to dictate, Let his guardian dictate faithfully, and get two witnesses, out of your own men, and if there are not two men, then a man and two women, such as ye choose, for witnesses, so that if one of them errs, the other can remind her. The witnesses should not refuse when they are called on (For evidence). Disdain not to reduce to writing (your contract) for a future period, whether it be small or big: it is juster in the sight of Allah, More suitable as evidence, and more convenient to prevent doubts among yourselves but if it be a transaction which ye carry out on the spot among yourselves, there is no blame on you if ye reduce it not to writing. But take witness whenever ye make a commercial contract; and let neither scribe nor witness suffer harm. If ye do (such harm), it would be wickedness in you. So fear Allah; For it is Good that teaches you. And Allah is well acquainted with all things.

The matter of inheritance in Islam let us not forget the unfairness of Islam towards women on this matter. Women get only half that men get.

Many Islamists justify this rule by saying that a woman does not contribute anything to the creation of a family wealth. All the money she gets is for hers to keep. It is a great tragedy to be born as a woman in an Islamic paradise.

In regard to the Muslim widows

4:12.

سورة النساء - سورة 4

WOMEN

وَلَكُمْ نِصْفُ مَا تَرَكَ أَزْوَاجُكُمْ إِن لَّمْ يَكُن لَّهُنَّ وَلَدٌ فَإِن كَانَ
لَهُنَّ وَلَدٌ فَلَكُمُ الرُّبُعُ مِمَّا تَرَكْنَ مِن بَعْدِ وَصِيَّةٍ يُوصِينَ بِهَا أَوْ
دَيْنٍ وَلَهُنَّ الرُّبُعُ مِمَّا تَرَكْتُمْ إِن لَّمْ يَكُن لَّكُمْ وَلَدٌ فَإِن كَانَ لَكُمْ
وَلَدٌ فَلَهُنَّ الثُّمُنُ مِمَّا تَرَكْتُم مِّن بَعْدِ وَصِيَّةٍ تُوصُونَ بِهَا أَوْ
دَيْنٍ وَإِن كَانَ رَجُلٌ يُورَثُ كَلاَلَةً أَو امْرَأَةٌ وَلَهُ أَخٌ أَوْ أُخْتٌ
فَلِكُلِّ وَاحِدٍ مِّنْهُمَا السُّدُسُ فَإِن كَانُوَاْ أَكْثَرَ مِن ذَلِكَ فَهُمْ
شُرَكَاء فِي الثُّلُثِ مِن بَعْدِ وَصِيَّةٍ يُوصَى بِهَآ أَوْ دَيْنٍ غَيْرَ
مُضَآرٍّ وَصِيَّةً مِّنَ اللّهِ وَاللّهُ عَلِيمٌ حَلِيمٌ

In what your wives leave, your share is a half, if they leave no child; but if they leave a child, ye get a fourth;

Muta System

Playboys, of the Muslim World, Islam have the solution even for them. It is very much in practice among the Shias. It is quite possible to have a Muta marriage every night and kick out the woman next morning.

There is no need of divorce in a Muta marriage. For all practical purposes, this type of marriage is a contract to sleep together and that is all.

Sunnis have banned the Muta marriage.

It should, be noted, that Sure 70:29-30, also revealed in Mecca, uses the identical words as 23:5-6.

70 سورة - الـمعارج سورة

THE ASCENDING STAIRWAYS

وَالَّذِينَ هُمْ لِفُرُوجِهِمْ حَافِظُونَ

إِلَّا عَلَى أَزْوَاجِهِمْ أَوْ مَا مَلَكَتْ أَيْمَانُهُمْ فَإِنَّهُمْ غَيْرُ مَلُومِينَ

And those who guard their chastity,
Except with their wives and the (captives) whom their right hands possess, for (then) they are not to be blamed

It seems that Muhammad utters meaningless statements. Men cheat on their wives, abandon them and divorce them for the most insignificant reasons or for no reason at all. It is nonsense to say that the majority of the people in the fires of hell are women because they curse each other and they do not acknowledge the merits of their husbands.

Here also we find gender discrimination. Another hadith says Men will enter into paradise after a short conversation with God. When Muslim men die and pass to Islamic Paradise, they expect to enter a utopian dimension where wine, milk and honey flows, fruit-trees flourish and rivers gush forth with the purist water.

Here, they plan to be greeted by 72 young virgins of "perpetual freshness" (houris) who will lead them into palaces loaded with luxurious thrones surrounded by gold, silver and jewel plated furnishings, a holy place where believers reclined on jewelled couches surrounded by the finest silks can experience unlimited erotic sexual pleasures.

Whatever Muhammad dreamed mostly young virgin girls for sex, thrones and wealth, he used it as a message from Allah. This shows how greedy and sexualised Muhammad was. His followers were like him so to take advantage of their greediness he promised them young virgin girls for sex, wealth etc in paradise.

Muhammad said the sensation that you feel each time you make love is utterly delicious and out of this world and were you to experience it in a world you would faint.

Islamic apologists often try to hide the extreme graphic description of sexual ecstasy in Islamic paradise by Muhammad.

Evil terrorist Muhammad adopted what he thought to be correct for himself. He had the talent how to build a force (army) for himself and other of his men sex was a weakness.

The ultimate pity is that the Muslim women are made to accept all this in the name of Islam and Allah.

Institute of Terrorism ISLAM

Muhammad never earned his living after he got married to Khadija. His wealthy wife who had financed him was dead and all her money was spent by Muhammad who had not worked a single day after his marriage with Khadija. He made a living as a bandit and a terrorist.

The original history proves that the very first and most successful Muslim terrorist was Muhammad, the prophet of Islam. Many Muslims are peace loving and are thoroughly disgusted about the acts of Islamic terrorism. Most Muslims do not know these historical facts about their own prophet.

Islam, built upon Muhammad's words and deeds. Many Muslims are unaware of the Quran's near absence of verses that preach non-violence. This is because their understanding of Islam comes from what they are taught. They are born Muslims and just follow the religion without going into depth.

We know it is disturbing for Muslims to read about Muhammad and Islam. It is indeed disturbing. However, it would be more disturbing if no one spoke about it.

Muhammad taught his followers to oppress or kill non-Muslims. Islam must rule the world. Muhammad wanted to kill all non-Muslims. Enslaved and controlled by Muslims. Muhammad gave in fact a License to Kill in the name of Allah.

Holy War is the holy law of Islam. This unique law called Jihad gives all Muslims the right to attack and kill non-Muslims, to loot, rape and enslave them, and to rule the world in the name of Allah.

Terrorism has existed in the world since Muhammad declared to be a prophet of Islam. Muslims are, brought up from early childhood to revere the prophet Muhammad and to honor him highly.

They are, commanded to hold his honor dearer than their own lives or those of their family members. If you insulted Muhammad, if you doubted his credibility and if you spoke out, you were murdered.

Muhammad came to power with his Muslim converts, a gang that developed into an army, attacking, killing, looting, enslaving and raping all of Arabia and then the infidel world, all in the name of Allah.

The so-called radicals, extremists, militants of today are in fact the real Muslims, who are obeying the laws of their Allah and the perfect example of their prophet.

Muslims are ordered to believe and who believed was the ideal human being. Muhammad was a bloodthirsty tyrant.

Islam is Institute Of Terrorism Madrasas & Masjeds

The seed of terrorism is, planted, deep within the theology of Islam. Muhammad said, "I have been ordered to fight against people until they say that "there is no God but Allah", that "Muhammad is the messenger of Allah", they pray, and pay religious taxes. If they do that, their lives and property are safe." Mohammad wanted everything under his control.

Islam

Islam was a convenient religious excuse for him to do this. Muslims believe that expansion through war is not aggression but a fulfillment of the Quran command to spread Islam.

Madrasas and Masjeds are Muslims religious educational institutions. These religious Institutions are giving Islamic education. So with this extremist and militancy education terrorist are born.

Islam is the breeding religion of fundamentalists and terrorists. The mullahs are playing a major role in this terrorist education. These fanatic mullahs are worse than the aids but are all over the world.

Islamic education must, be banned, in the world especially in non-Islamic countries. Muslims specially mullahs must be rounded up and sent to Islamic countries.

Girls and women should be aware of these terrorist Muslims so they should not marry them for Immigration. Muslim men, take advantage, of non-Muslim women specially girls, they marry them, take immigration and their children then runaway.

Sure: (8): 12, 57, and 67.

سورة الأنفال - سورة 8

SPOILS OF WAR

(12)

إِذْ يُوحِي رَبُّكَ إِلَى الْمَلآئِكَةِ أَنِّي مَعَكُمْ فَثَبِّتُواْ الَّذِينَ آمَنُواْ
سَأُلْقِي فِي قُلُوبِ الَّذِينَ كَفَرُواْ الرَّعْبَ فَاضْرِبُواْ فَوْقَ الأَعْنَاقِ
وَاضْرِبُواْ مِنْهُمْ كُلَّ بَنَانٍ

Remember thy Lord inspired the angels (with the message): "I am with you: give firmness to the Believers: I will instill terror into the hearts of the Unbelievers: smite ye above their necks and smite all their finger-tips off them."

(57)

فَإِمَّا تَثْقَفَنَّهُمْ فِي الْحَرْبِ فَشَرِّدْ بِهِم مَّنْ خَلْفَهُمْ لَعَلَّهُمْ يَذَّكَّرُونَ

If ye gain the mastery over them in war, disperse, with them, those who follow them, that they may remember.

(67)

مَا كَانَ لِنَبِيٍّ أَن يَكُونَ لَهُ أَسْرَى حَتَّى يُثْخِنَ فِي الأَرْضِ
تُرِيدُونَ عَرَضَ الدُّنْيَا وَاللّهُ يُرِيدُ الآخِرَةَ وَاللّهُ عَزِيزٌ حَكِيمٌ

It is not fitting for an apostle that he should have prisoners of war until he hath thoroughly subdued the land. Ye look for the temporal goods of this world; but Allah looketh to the Hereafter: And Allah is Exalted in might, Wise.

Sure: (9): 5, 14, 19, 29, 38, 112, and 123.

سورة التوبة - سورة 9

REPENTANCE

(14)

وَمِنَ الَّذِينَ قَالُواْ إِنَّا نَصَارَى أَخَذْنَا مِيثَاقَهُمْ فَنَسُواْ حَظًّا مِّمَّا ذُكِّرُواْ بِهِ فَأَغْرَيْنَا بَيْنَهُمُ الْعَدَاوَةَ وَالْبَغْضَاء إِلَى يَوْمِ الْقِيَامَةِ وَسَوْفَ يُنَبِّئُهُمُ اللّهُ بِمَا كَانُواْ يَصْنَعُونَ

From those, too, who call themselves Christians, We did take a covenant, but they forgot a good part of the message that was sent them: so we estranged them, with enmity and hatred between the one and the other, to the day of judgment. And soon will Allah show them what it is they have done.

(19)

يَا أَهْلَ الْكِتَابِ قَدْ جَاءكُمْ رَسُولُنَا يُبَيِّنُ لَكُمْ عَلَى فَتْرَةٍ مِّنَ الرُّسُلِ أَن تَقُولُواْ مَا جَاءنَا مِن بَشِيرٍ وَلاَ نَذِيرٍ فَقَدْ جَاءكُم بَشِيرٌ وَنَذِيرٌ وَاللّهُ عَلَى كُلِّ شَيْءٍ قَدِيرٌ

O People of the Book! Now hath come unto you, making (things) clear unto you, Our Messenger, after the break in (the series of) our apostles, lest ye should say: "There came unto us no bringer of glad tidings and no warner (from evil)": But now hath come unto you a bringer of glad tidings and a warner (from evil). And Allah hath power over all things.

(29)

إِنِّي أُرِيدُ أَن تَبُوءَ بِإِثْمِي وَإِثْمِكَ فَتَكُونَ مِنْ أَصْحَابِ النَّارِ
وَذَلِكَ جَزَاء الظَّالِمِينَ

"For me, I intend to let thee draw on thyself my sin as well as thine, for thou wilt be among the companions of the fire, and that is the reward of those who do wrong."

(88)

لَـكِنِ الرَّسُولُ وَالَّذِينَ آمَنُواْ مَعَهُ جَاهَدُواْ بِأَمْوَالِهِمْ وَأَنفُسِهِمْ
وَأُوْلَـئِكَ لَهُمُ الْخَيْرَاتُ وَأُوْلَـئِكَ هُمُ الْمُفْلِحُونَ

But the Apostle, and those who believe with him, strive and fight with their wealth and their persons: for them are (all) good things: and it is they who will prosper.

A lot more is to written, in next vole, on the sinfulness of Muhammad. It is true that many Muslims do not believe, rather, they prefer an idealized and fictional prophet of their own imagination.

96: 1-4

سورة 69 - سورة الـ عـ لق

READ

اقْرَأْ بِاسْمِ رَبِّكَ الَّذِي خَلَقَ

Proclaim! (or read!) in the name of thy Lord and Cherisher, Who created

الَّذِي عَلَّمَ بِالْقَلَمِ

He Who taught (the use of) the pen

8 سورة 6 - سورة الـ قـ لم

THE PEN

ن وَالْقَلَمِ وَمَا يَسْطُرُونَ

Nun. By the Pen and the (Record) which (men) write

Pakistan is doing the same, collecting money (Donations) to help the needy but less than 10/12% is spend on them rest is to use against non Muslims.(Nuclear power, protecting Osama bin Laden etc)

Muhammad was master in dramatising so are the followers. He fooled of being illiterate which he was not.

Halal and Haram

Halal is an Arabic word to describe things that are lawful, for Muslims and Haram is the opposite, which means unlawful.

Muhammad always concentrated on the life style that is different from others. He thought off all those strategies that made Muslims different from other religions although he took a lot from other religions. Muhammad believed that he has a divine right from his Allah to impose his will on others.

He told people Islam is superior to all religions.

Muhammad always tried to keep Muslims under full control. He established certain legal principles and measures for rectifying him and his Allah is important. These principles were then, made the determining criteria on which the questions of what is halal and what is haram were to be based.

The concept of Halal and Haram in Islam is very clear. This principle is a part of discrimination between Muslims and nonmuslims, that great trust which Muslims accepted. Islamic education teaches double standard, one for Muslims and another for non-Muslims or outsider but they expect them to treat like all other citizens in non-Muslim countries.

Allah says Muslims will become Mushriks, because Muslims will associate these people with Allah in giving Muslims commands.

This verse deals with hunting for meat. Allah has commanded Muslims to recite His name before letting loose the hunting animals (e.g., dogs, hawks, etc.) after the pray. Only then, the hunted animal will be Halal; otherwise, it will be Haram. This law of hunting has been, mentioned very clearly in many hadith as well. This is the only right way to make sure the hunt is Halal.

6:118

سورة الأنعام - سورة 6

LIVESTOCK

فَكُلُواْ مِمَّا ذُكِرَ اسْمُ اللّهِ عَلَيْهِ إِن كُنتُمْ بِآيَاتِهِ مُؤْمِنِينَ

So eat of (meats) on which Allah's name hath been pronounced, if ye have faith in His signs.

Halal and Haram are part of the system of Islam, its Sharia. Halal and haram in the Islamic Sharia

Slaughtering by cutting the throat

Muhammad did not even spared animals, he told his followers to, ritually slaughter animals whose blood has left their bodies while dying. He taught that it would be a good thing to sedate the animals before cutting their throats. In that case, it takes 10 to 20 seconds before the animal is unconscious because of lack of oxygen. That slaughtering the animal with any sharp object makes it Halal.

is sacrificed on stone (altars); (forbidden) also is the division (of meat) by raffling with arrows: that is impiety. This day have those who reject faith given up all hope of your religion: yet fear them not but fear Me. This day have I perfected your religion for you, completed my favors upon you, and have chosen for you Islam as your religion. But if any is forced by hunger, with no inclination to transgression, Allah is indeed Oft forgiving, Most Merciful

يَسْأَلُونَكَ مَاذَا أُحِلَّ لَهُمْ قُلْ أُحِلَّ لَكُمُ الطَّيِّبَاتُ وَمَا عَلَّمْتُم مِّنَ الْجَوَارِحِ مُكَلِّبِينَ تُعَلِّمُونَهُنَّ مِمَّا عَلَّمَكُمُ اللّهُ فَكُلُواْ مِمَّا أَمْسَكْنَ عَلَيْكُمْ وَاذْكُرُواْ اسْمَ اللّهِ عَلَيْهِ وَاتَّقُواْ اللّهَ إِنَّ اللّهَ سَرِيعُ الْحِسَابِ

They ask thee what is lawful to them (as food). Say: lawful unto you are (all) things good and pure: and what

For Muslims it is haram to slaughter an animal in a name other than Allah but halal to slaughter a human being in the name of Allah. It is haram for a woman to have more than one husband but halal for a husband to have more than one wife.

For Muhammad it was halal to marry an underage child Aisha, kill non-Muslims and sleep with their wives and daughters. In Islam, it is haram for a wife to refuse her husband even she is, occupied at the oven but halal for a husband to beat her.

Muslims identify themselves as Muslim first and then any other nationality

There is no peaceful Islam, there is only one Islam and that is what we see today, if we do not open our eyes this terrorist, religion will close our eyes forever.

Islamic culture lacks the words to, properly explain what they are thinking or meaning because their religion tells them to kill and create terror in the heart of non-Muslims but they are hiding the truth, they cover by saying Islam is a religion of peace. Islam does not means peace it means submission. Muhammad taught that give your life to Muhammad in the name of Allah.

Muslims does not respect for human life.The Muslims are from the worst religion that have crept into western countries, lying low until they get the opportunity to fulfill their religion duties.

They pretend to live in peace but their hidden agenda is something quite different. Let all the Islamists live in the Islamic states.

Muslims claim falsely universal unity, fellowship between Muslim and Muslim, not any person of another community. Muslims religion does not allow them to be friendly with non-Muslims.

Nuclear-armed Pakistan is a support for terrorism leaders. The fact is that Islamic countries are the very countries that spew hate, every Friday at their Mosques to kill all non-believers; it is the lesson of their religion.

Muhammad, a son of man, says to kill your enemies.

Jesus, the Son of God, says we are to love our enemies.

Islam is not giving respect to Muslim women what respect can Islam give to others. Muhammad grew up with a lack of love of a mother so first he married 15-year-older than him, a rich women who took care of him, he did not had to work after marriage.

Muhammad was a womanizer but was afraid of mummy like wife so he started going in a cave far from the place they lived, to satisfy his lust for sex, but he had to find an excuse for that so he planned a good fortune for him by dramatizing of revolutions from Allah and did propaganda of a Prophet.

Most individual Muslims may respect and honor women, because as we wrote before that, most of Muslims are just born Muslims unaware of the reality of the teachings of Islam. They just are aware of praying and reading Quran. They do not understand because from their childhood they are not allow to question, think or even talk against Muhammad or his teachings. Islam does not respect humanity and off course women.

The Islamic Quran itself is responsible for cruelty toward Muslim women, both young and old. The syllabus of Islam or we can say the evil book of Muhammad calls woman a field or a tilth. This field is to be, used by a Muslim man as he sees fit. Muhammad himself was the model of what he said and how he treated women.

2:223

سورة البقرة - سورة 2

THE COW

نِسَآؤُكُمْ حَرْثٌ لَّكُمْ فَأْتُواْ حَرْثَكُمْ أَنَّى شِئْتُمْ وَقَدِّمُواْ لأَنفُسِكُمْ وَاتَّقُواْ اللّهَ وَاعْلَمُواْ أَنَّكُم مُّلاَقُوهُ وَبَشِّرِ الْمُؤْمِنِينَ

Your wives are as a tilth unto you; so approach your tilth when or how ye will; but do some good act for your souls beforehand; and fear Allah. And know that ye are to meet Him (in the Hereafter), and give (these) good tidings to those who believe.

Errors in Quran Who is the liar? Muhammad or Allah

It is not insulting to except that we were at mistake, insulting is when one cannot prove that he was not at fault. Greatness and respect is to except that we were on wrong path because we were not fully aware of the reality but changed and adopted the right path.

We (Asma Shah & Manjeet Singh) are not making any decision for the Muslims. We are the victims of this religion. We want to open the eyes of all, no matter Muslims or non-Muslims. We want the world to be aware of the reality and the errors of a liar, so called Prophet Muhammad.

Muslims believe that the Quran is infallible and inerrant. Quran contains no errors, no logical fallacies, perfect ethics and signs of future science. We have copied the verses of Quran from the Quran

Read it, and...

In Quran, 15:26 it says man made from clay. In 21:30, it says man made from water. Moreover, in 96:1-2 we read that God made man from a blood clot.

15:26

سورة 51 - سورة الا حجر

AL-HIJR

وَلَقَدْ خَلَقْنَا الإِنسَانَ مِن صَلْصَالٍ مِّنْ حَمَإٍ مَّسْنُونٍ

We created man from sounding clay, from mud moulded into shape

21:30

سورة 12 - سورة الأذ ب ياء

THE PROPHETS

أَوَلَمْ يَرَ الَّذِينَ كَفَرُوا أَنَّ السَّمَاوَاتِ وَالْأَرْضَ كَانَتَا رَتْقًا فَفَتَقْنَاهُمَا وَجَعَلْنَا مِنَ الْمَاء كُلَّ شَيْءٍ حَيٍّ أَفَلَا يُؤْمِنُونَ

Do not the Unbelievers see that the heavens and the earth were joined together (as one unit of creation), before we clove them asunder? We made from water every living thing. Will they not then believe?

96:1-2

سورة 69 - سورة الـ عـ لق

THE CLOT

اقْرَأْ بِاسْمِ رَبِّكَ الَّذِي خَلَقَ

خَلَقَ الْإِنسَانَ مِنْ عَلَقٍ

Proclaim! (or read!) in the name of thy Lord and Cherisher, Who created-

Created man, out of a (mere) clot of congealed blood:

Creation of Heaven and Earth, 2:29 says first earth and then heaven was, created. However, 79:27-30 indicate, first heaven was created, and after that earth.

سورة البقرة - سورة 2

THE COW

هُوَ الَّذِي خَلَقَ لَكُم مَّا فِي الأَرْضِ جَمِيعاً ثُمَّ اسْتَوَى إِلَى
السَّمَاء فَسَوَّاهُنَّ سَبْعَ سَمَاوَاتٍ وَهُوَ بِكُلِّ شَيْءٍ عَلِيمٌ

It is He Who hath created for you all things that are on earth; Moreover His design comprehended the heavens, for He gave order and perfection to the seven firmaments; and of all things He hath perfect knowledge.

79:27-30

سورة 97 - سورة الـ نازعات

THOSE WHO DRAG FORTH

أَأَنتُمْ أَشَدُّ خَلْقًا أَمِ السَّمَاء بَنَاهَا

What! Are ye the more difficult to create or the heaven (above)? (Allah) hath constructed it

30

وَالْأَرْضَ بَعْدَ ذَلِكَ دَحَاهَا

And the earth, moreover, hath He extended

In 2:234, widows are to keep themselves apart for 4 months and 10 days after their husband's death. In 2:240, it is one year.

2:234

سورة البقرة - سورة 2

THE COW

وَالَّذِينَ يُتَوَفَّوْنَ مِنكُمْ وَيَذَرُونَ أَزْوَاجًا يَتَرَبَّصْنَ بِأَنفُسِهِنَّ أَرْبَعَةَ أَشْهُرٍ وَعَشْرًا فَإِذَا بَلَغْنَ أَجَلَهُنَّ فَلاَ جُنَاحَ عَلَيْكُمْ فِيمَا فَعَلْنَ فِي أَنفُسِهِنَّ بِالْمَعْرُوفِ وَاللّهُ بِمَا تَعْمَلُونَ خَبِيرٌ

If any of you die and leave widows behind, they shall wait concerning themselves four months and ten days: When they have fulfilled their term, there is no blame on you if they dispose of themselves in a just and reasonable manner. And Allah is well acquainted with what ye do.

5:69

سورة المائدة - سورة 5

THE TABLE

إِنَّ الَّذِينَ آمَنُواْ وَالَّذِينَ هَادُواْ وَالصَّابِؤُونَ وَالنَّصَارَى مَنْ
آمَنَ بِاللّهِ وَالْيَوْمِ الآخِرِ وعَمِلَ صَالِحًا فَلاَ خَوْفٌ عَلَيْهِمْ وَلاَ
هُمْ يَحْزَنُونَ

Those who believe (in the Qur'an), those who follow the Jewish (scriptures), and the Sabians and the Christians,- any who believe in Allah and the Last Day, and work righteousness,- on them shall be no fear, nor shall they grieve.

3:85

سورة آل عمران - سورة 3

THE FAMILY OF IMRAN

وَمَن يَبْتَغِ غَيْرَ الإِسْلاَمِ دِينًا فَلَن يُقْبَلَ مِنْهُ وَهُوَ فِي الآخِرَةِ مِنَ الْخَاسِرِينَ

If anyone desires a religion other than Islam (submission to Allah), never will it be accepted of him; and in the Hereafter He will be in the ranks of those who have lost (All spiritual good)

5:72

سورة المائدة - سورة 5

THE TABLE

لَقَدْ كَفَرَ الَّذِينَ قَالُواْ إِنَّ اللّهَ هُوَ الْمَسِيحُ ابْنُ مَرْيَمَ وَقَالَ الْمَسِيحُ
يَا بَنِي إِسْرَائِيلَ اعْبُدُواْ اللّهَ رَبِّي وَرَبَّكُمْ إِنَّهُ مَن يُشْرِكْ بِاللّهِ
فَقَدْ حَرَّمَ اللّهُ عَلَيهِ الْجَنَّةَ وَمَأْوَاهُ النَّارُ وَمَا لِلظَّالِمِينَ مِنْ
أَنصَارٍ

They do blaspheme who say: "(Allah) is Christ the son of Mary." But said Christ: "O Children of Israel! worship Allah, my Lord and your Lord." Whoever joins other gods with Allah, - Allah will forbid him the garden, and the Fire will be his abode. There will for the wrong-doers be no one to help

Wine: Bad to drink when alive but served in Paradise.

One side he says wine is not good but why will Wine, be, served in Paradise. Simple, Muhammad was cleaver and his weakness was women and drinks so the people who followed him had the same. To fool them he said they would get all they wanted in Paradise because if they drank in the world, how will they fight.

2:219 and 5:90-91. Strong drinks are infamy of Satan's handiwork. 47:15, and 83: 22, 25 But on the other hand in Paradise are rivers of wine. Why Satan's handiworks get into Paradise?

2:219 also says there is profit in intoxicants.

2:219

سورة البقرة - سورة 2

THE COW

يَسْأَلُونَكَ عَنِ الْخَمْرِ وَالْمَيْسِرِ قُلْ فِيهِمَا إِثْمٌ كَبِيرٌ وَمَنَافِعُ
لِلنَّاسِ وَإِثْمُهُمَآ أَكْبَرُ مِن نَّفْعِهِمَا وَيَسْأَلُونَكَ مَاذَا يُنفِقُونَ قُلِ
الْعَفْوَ كَذَلِكَ يُبيِّنُ اللّهُ لَكُمُ الآيَاتِ لَعَلَّكُمْ تَتَفَكَّرُونَ

They ask thee concerning wine and gambling. Say: "In them is great sin, and some profit, for men; but the sin is greater than the profit." They ask thee how much they are to spend; Say: "What is beyond your needs." Thus doth Allah Make clear to you His Signs: In order that ye may consider

5:90-91

سورة المائدة - سورة 5

THE TABLE

يَا أَيُّهَا الَّذِينَ آمَنُواْ إِنَّمَا الْخَمْرُ وَالْمَيْسِرُ وَالأَنصَابُ وَالأَزْلاَمُ
رِجْسٌ مِّنْ عَمَلِ الشَّيْطَانِ فَاجْتَنِبُوهُ لَعَلَّكُمْ تُفْلِحُونَ

O ye who believe! Intoxicants and gambling, (dedication of) stones, and (divination by) arrows, are an abomination, - of Satan's handwork: eschew such (abomination), that ye may prosper.

91

إِنَّمَا يُرِيدُ الشَّيْطَانُ أَن يُوقِعَ بَيْنَكُمُ الْعَدَاوَةَ وَالْبَغْضَاء فِي الْخَمْرِ وَالْمَيْسِرِ وَيَصُدَّكُمْ عَن ذِكْرِ اللّهِ وَعَنِ الصَّلاَةِ فَهَلْ أَنتُم مُّنتَهُونَ

Satan's plan is (but) to excite enmity and hatred between you, with intoxicants and gambling, and hinder you from the remembrance of Allah, and from prayer: will ye not then abstain?

47:15

سورة 74 - سورة محمد

MUHAMMAD

مَثَلُ الْجَنَّةِ الَّتِي وُعِدَ الْمُتَّقُونَ فِيهَا أَنْهَارٌ مِّن مَّاء غَيْرِ آسِنٍ وَأَنْهَارٌ مِن لَّبَنٍ لَّمْ يَتَغَيَّرْ طَعْمُهُ وَأَنْهَارٌ مِّنْ خَمْرٍ لَّذَّةٍ لِّلشَّارِبِينَ وَأَنْهَارٌ مِّنْ عَسَلٍ مُّصَفًّى وَلَهُمْ فِيهَا مِن كُلِّ الثَّمَرَاتِ وَمَغْفِرَةٌ مِّن رَّبِّهِمْ كَمَنْ هُوَ خَالِدٌ فِي النَّارِ وَسُقُوا مَاء حَمِيمًا فَقَطَّعَ أَمْعَاءهُمْ

(Here is) a Parable of the Garden which the righteous are promised: in it are rivers of water incorruptible; rivers of milk of which the taste never changes; rivers of wine, a joy to those who drink; and rivers of honey pure and clear. In it, there are for them all kinds of fruits; and Grace from their Lord. (Can those in such Bliss) be compared to such as shall dwell forever in the Fire, and be given, to drink, boiling water, so that it cuts up their bowels (to pieces)?

83: 22, 25

سورة 38 - سورة الـمطـ ف ف ين

DEFRAUDING

إِنَّ الْأَبْرَارَ لَفِي نَعِيمٍ

Truly the Righteous will be in Bliss:

25

يُسْقَوْنَ مِن رَّحِيقٍ مَّخْتُومٍ

Their thirst will be slaked with Pure Wine sealed:

The change of Kibla From Jerusalem To Kaba

The Quraysh tribe prayed to idols at sunrise, noon, and at sunset in Kaba. Muhammad started merchandising at the age of nine. While away from Arabia, he saw the sacred places of the Jews. He saw Damascus, city of the desert, and Sinai, the mountain of the law. Then he returned to Mecca with dreams. At the age of 20, Muhammad was, hired by a wealthy woman named Khadijah to manage her late husband's caravan business. At the age of 25 Muhammad married her and was rich, now he was able to fulfill his dreams. He was well aware of the position and states of Jews, so he thought of fooling them first this was the reason of praying towards the Jerusalem.

Muhammad tried his best to appease Jews and Christians in the hope of convincing them that he was a true prophet. He even adopted certain Jewish and Christian practices such as fasting, dietary restrictions etc.

When he saw that, the Jews and Christians were not accepting his prophetic claims. He saw and observed the power and strength of Jews he changed Kibla from Jerusalem to Kaba. Muhammad turned against them. This is the reason that once Koran says yes, they will go to Paradise and then no.

Allah is Muhammad and Muhammad is Allah this is the reason when Muhammad take a step Allah sends the conformation through so-called Gabriel.

Allah is defending himself, or Muhammad is defending Allah, whichever way one may look at it. Quran, reference for first Kibla and the new Kibla:

2:137

سورة البقرة - سورة 2

THE COW

فَإِنْ آمَنُواْ بِمِثْلِ مَا آمَنتُم بِهِ فَقَدِ اهْتَدَواْ وَّإِن تَوَلَّوْاْ فَإِنَّمَا هُمْ فِي شِقَاقٍ فَسَيَكْفِيكَهُمُ اللّهُ وَهُوَ السَّمِيعُ الْعَلِيمُ

So if they believe as ye believe, they are indeed on the right path; but if they turn back, it is they who are in schism; but Allah will suffice thee as against them, and He is the All-Hearing, the All-Knowing

142

سَيَقُولُ السُّفَهَاء مِنَ النَّاسِ مَا وَلاَّهُمْ عَن قِبْلَتِهِمُ الَّتِي كَانُواْ عَلَيْهَا قُل لِّلّهِ الْمَشْرِقُ وَالْمَغْرِبُ يَهْدِي مَن يَشَاء إِلَى صِرَاطٍ مُّسْتَقِيمٍ

The fools among the people will say: "What hath turned them from the Qibla to which they were used?" Say:

To Allah belong both east and West:
He guideth whom He will to a Way
that is straight

144

قَدْ نَرَى تَقَلُّبَ وَجْهِكَ فِي السَّمَاء فَلَنُوَلِّيَنَّكَ قِبْلَةً تَرْضَاهَا فَوَلِّ
وَجْهَكَ شَطْرَ الْمَسْجِدِ الْحَرَامِ وَحَيْثُ مَا كُنتُمْ فَوَلُّواْ وُجُوِهَكُمْ
شَطْرَهُ وَإِنَّ الَّذِينَ أُوْتُواْ الْكِتَابَ لَيَعْلَمُونَ أَنَّهُ الْحَقُّ مِن رَّبِّهِمْ
وَمَا اللّهُ بِغَافِلٍ عَمَّا يَعْمَلُونَ

We see the turning of thy face (for guidance to the heavens: now Shall We turn thee to a Qibla that shall please thee. Turn then Thy face in the direction of the sacred Mosque: Wherever ye are, turn your faces in that direction. The people of the Book know well that that is the truth from their Lord. Nor is Allah unmindful of what they do

Sikhs and Muslims

Islam means submission or surrender to the will of Muhammad and Allah. Sikh means learner. Learner means student who learn from their teachers. Teachers are Gurus. Sikh is Student of Gurus.

Sikhism is a complete religion but unknown to those who think Sikhism is an attempt to harmonize two religions, Hinduism and Islam. Guru Nanak, the founder of Sikhism he did a close study on Islamic literature.

Guru Nanak Dev Ji was not a Muslim. Nanak preached that life is real and not Maya or

of Guru Nanak, Babar seemed to come under a magic spell.

Since the Emperor did not comprehend the words of the holy song, he asked Guru Nanak for a translation. The Guru boldly told him that he was singing about the cruelty of the Emperor and the sad state of the victims. Impressed by Guru Nanak's courage, Babar freed the prisoners.

Guru Nanak in his famous epic named Babarbani describes the atrocities of Babar and his men in Punjab. Muslims of South Asia are descendants of weaker elements of the population who had succumbed to forcible Islamic conversion. The Islamic scholars have recorded with pride of the slaughters of Hindus, forced conversions, abduction of Hindu women and children to slave markets and the destruction of temples carried out by the warriors of Islam.

Millions of Hindus and Sikhs converted to Islam by sword during that period. Hindus and Sikhs were the victims of one of the bloodiest holocausts of world history. They were, forcefully converted to Islam.

Once when Guru Nanak was, asked which religion, Hinduism or Islam was the true path to God, Guru Nanak replied that the true way to attain God was to worship Him who is eternal and contained in the whole Universe.

Guru Nanak traveled for 21 long years imparting his wisdom wherever he set foot. He arrived in Mecca after an exhausting journey. To rest his weary feet he lay down. The Muslims saw him took great offence when they noticed that the Guru's feet were pointing towards the Kaba.

Muslims, kicked the Guru in anger and said why your feet are facing Allah, they demanded an explanation. The Guru benevolently smiled and said that turn his feet where there is no Allah. The Guru had once again imparted an immortal lesson. The Lord resides in every place and in every heart.

When Guru Nanak merged into the eternal light, the Hindus wanted to cremate him while the Muslims wanted to bury the body. However, on raising the sheet under which the Great Guru's body lay, both found nothing but fresh flowers that were, divided between them. The Hindus cremated the flowers whereas the Muslims buried theirs. Like Guru, Nanak claims in one of his hymns:

'Nanak leen bhayo Govind syon
Jyon pani sang pani'

Meaning, that Guru Nanak has so merged, with the Lord, like water with water.

Five physical signs identify Khalsa.

The five K:

1. Kesh (uncut hair),
2. Kanga (a wooden comb),
3. Kkaccha (shorts worn under regular clothes),
4. Kara (a steel bracelet), and
5. Kirpan (short sword, not for violence).

These members, when initiated, take on a new surname: Singh (lion) for the men, and Kaur (princess) for the women this group is highly revered among the Sikhs for their commitment.

Founding Of The Khalsa

The Khalsa Panth militarized to form a political and military bloc against the aggression of the Islamic Mughal Empire.

After the death of his father Mughal Emperor Akbar, Jahangir became the Emperor of the Mughals. Jahangir was jealous about Guru's propagation of Sikhism. Jahangir was a fundamentalist Muslim, obsessed into turning the country into an Islamic state.

Many allegations were, leveled against the Guru, one of those was helping the rebellious Khusrau, who was Jahangir's son and determined to rule Punjab.

In Late May 1606, Guru Arjan Dev was, arrested and brought to Lahore where he was subject to severe torture. He was, made to sit on a burning hot plate while hot sand poured over his head and body. It is, said that Mian Mir (a Muslim Sufi Saint and friend of the Guru) tried to intercede on behalf of the Guru but he forbade him to interfere. Guru was, subjected to torture.

Early in the reign of the Mughal emperor Aurangzeb's, various insurgent groups of Sikhs engaged Mughal troops in increasingly bloody battles. In 1670, the ninth Sikh Guru, Guru Tegh Bahadur encamped in Delhi, receiving large numbers of followers.

Aurangzeb regarded this popularity as a potential threat, and determined to subdue it. Kashmiri Brahmins, who were of the Hindu faith, were being, pressured by Muslim authorities to convert to Islam and approached Guru Tegh Bahadur with their dilemma.

To demonstrate a spirit of unity and tolerance, the Guru agreed to help the Brahmins: He told them to inform Aurangzeb that the Brahmins would convert only if Guru Tegh Bahadur himself was converted.

His response led to his death.

The Guru and his disciples tortured by various methods, boiled alive, and burned alive, sawn in half and scalped. Aurangzeb decided to try all brutal, methods to force Tegh Bahadur Sahib to accept Islam.

He was kept in, chains and imprisoned for three days in an iron cage designed to be shorter than the prisoner's height, with sharp spikes pointing inwards, so that the victim could neither stand, nor sit, nor lean against the walls of the cage. His execution infuriated the Sikhs. In response, his son and successor, Guru Gobind Singh further militarized his followers.

Aurangzeb installed his son Bahadur Shah as governor of the Northwest Territories, including Sikh-controlled parts of Punjab. Guru Gobind Singh had determined that the Sikhs should actively prepare to defend their territories and their faith. In 1699, he established the Khalsa a Sikh order of "saint-soldiers", ready to die for their cause.

This development alarmed the Mughals. Mughals attacked Guru Gobind Singh and his followers. The united Mughal armies laid siege to the fort at

Anandpur Sahib. Although they faced certain death, the Sikhs refused to surrender.

In an attempt to dislodge the Sikhs, Aurangzeb vowed that the Guru and his Sikhs be allowed to leave Anandpur safely.

Aurangzeb validated this promise in writing. Unconfirmed by scholars, this account of the promise is unlikely; however, seeing the suffering of his followers, Guru Gobind Singh Ji had made plans to sneak away. It is, reported that in, the absence of any formal surrender by the Sikhs, as they abandoned the fort under the cover of darkness, the Mughals were alerted and engaged the battle to ensue again.

The Mughals, although suffering some mighty losses, apparently killed all four of Guru Gobind Singh's sons and decimated much of the Sikh army. Only Guru Gobind Singh and forty brave Sikhs escaped. Guru Gobind Singh in response sent Aurangzeb an eloquent yet defiant letter entitled the Zafarnama (Notification of Victory), accusing the emperor of treachery, and claiming a moral victory. On receipt of this letter, Aurangzeb is, said to have invited Guru Gobind Singh to meet in Ahmednagar, but Aurangzeb died before Guru Gobind Singh arrived.

The eighteenth century, various Khalsa groups fought the Mughals and Afghans.

Sikhs faced more political Problem In 1947, when Hindustan divided into two parts. The Sikhs and their homeland split in half by the boundaries. Sikhs, fleeing to India, were then separated from many of their most revered and historical sites occupied by Pakistan.

Muslims want to occupy the world through terrorist activities. They think they and their religion is powerful, they are at mistake because Islam is not spreading through spiritual strength, they are spreading Islam by killing other religions.

Pakistanis are taking advantage of Gurdawaras the holy palaces of Sikhs. Ukaf the Muslim organization for Muslim holy places takes the Chrawas, given to Gurdawaras by Sikhs all over the world.

I know Sikhs teach the truth to children but they should warn them of the danger of Islam and Muslim society because I Manjeet Singh I have suffered and I do not want any other to safer. Islam has only one goal in life and that is to convert non-Muslims by force and make lives miserable.

Content

Guru Nanak Dev Ji

Guru Nanak was not like Muhammad, who spread Islam by force and power. Guru Nanak Dev himself was a victim and an eyewitness to the havoc created during the invasions of Babar. Babar, the Muslim, mughal Emperor. Pakistanis are taking advantage of Gurdawaras the holy palaces of Sikhs. Ukaf the Muslim organization for Muslim holy places takes the Chrawas, given to Gurdawaras by Sikhs all over the world

Hindu Lord Shiva

Kaba shrine is a pre-Islamic Hindu Shiva Temple where the Hindu practice of circumambulation, still meticulously observed. The practice of taking seven steps known as Saptapadi in Sanskrit is associated with Hindu marriage ceremony and fire worship. Muslims cannot do Hajj until they kiss the black stone, which is a piece of the Idol Lord Shiva. This shows the power of Lord Shiva that without his permission they cannot go around his temple.

Hindu Lord Shiva
The Trishul in hand of the Lord
Is like the Arabic text ALLAH

We dedicate this book to all those who were victims and their families, which were, affected by the terrorist attacks of Muhammad through his terrorist Islamic education

ASMA SHAH

MANJEET SINGH

www.ingramcontent.com/pod-product-compliance
Ingram Content Group UK Ltd.
Pitfield, Milton Keynes, MK11 3LW, UK
UKHW041941190726
13854UKWH00004B/1728

9 781425 132132